# Diary of the White Bush Clover

## A Peace Pilgrimage

I0143061

GOTO HIROKO

CARE CONNET

1st WORLD PUBLISHING

Diary of the White Bush Clover

Goto Hiroko and Care Connet

Published by 1st World Publishing
P.O. Box 2211, Fairfield, Iowa 52556
tel: 641-209-5000 • fax: 866-440-5234
web: www.1stworldpublishing.com

First Edition

LCCN: 2014947896
Softcover ISBN: 978-1-59540-928-7
Hardcover ISBN: 978-1-59540-927-0
eBook ISBN: 978-1-59540-944-7

# Praise for *Diary of the White Bush Clover*

*Diary of the White Bush Clover* is a walking meditation into the power of kindness and the potency of immanent danger. The teachings of the Buddha evoke the power of grace that reflects a constancy of surprise. The reader is asked to partake in the daily discipline of pilgrimage that mirrors the repetitive character of mind. The purpose of meditation from this perspective is not only to stop attention from wandering but to enter a place where the clarity of pure awareness peeks through the instability of confusion. Through the power of Goto Hiroko's commitment, prescient landmarks impress the inner traveler with a steady eye that defies obstacles and melts despair. This spiritual journey is not undertaken on the seat of a cushion but with the increase of resolve that coincides with the gradual wearing down of one pair of sneakers. Both the delicacy and ferocity of nature are represented, holding the reader's concentration so that fears are gently tamed.

—Janet Sussman, author of *The Reality of Time*

Goto Hiroko's memoir, *Diary of the White Bush Clover*, reads like the best Japanese poetry. Her story is larger than she is, revealing the soul of the Japanese people, a nation wounded by a terrible war. As she tells us what she saw and felt while walking from Kyoto to Tokyo, her writing is so transparent that you enter the pages and walk with her. In the tradition of the haiku, she uses images of nature to reveal depth, emotion and vision – moments of beauty savored and celebrated, heaven and earth, despite having traveled through difficult times. She tosses gifts of spiritual awakening to her readers, like the Zen saying, "If you scoop water you hold the moon in your hands."

—Diane Frank, author of *Blackberries in the Dreamhouse*

This diary is a peace poem. Written in spare, lyrical simplicity, each chapter bestows gifts of wisdom and beauty to the reader. The haiku and calligraphy add layers of enchantment to this humble account of a great act of compassion. As I followed Goto Hiroko's journey I felt the world becoming a more peaceful place.

—Linda Egenes, author of *Visits with the Amish: Impressions of the Plain Life*

This diary and the elegant poems that punctuate this pilgrimage are subtle, beautiful and meaningful as breath. One cannot do better on one's journey than to be "a servant of life."

—Rustin Larson, author of *Waiting for Evening to Come*

At some point, those touched by war try to make sense of it, though there is no true sense to be made. Even so, a work and a pilgrimage such as this, in its careful cadences, brings peace, honor and loving attention back into the world. Reading the transliteration, translation and the narration of the poetry walks you step by step through a healing, silent field.

—Paul Stokstad, author of *Butterfly Tattoo*

*To those who died in war and those who live for peace.*

# CONTENTS

# PREFACE

I first met Goto Hiroko in the spring of 2000, an auspicious beginning to the new millennium. I was part of a group from Fairfield, Iowa, who had been invited for a home-stay as guests of Goto-san's International Cultural Academy, a visit that turned out to be part of my spiritual journey.

Goto Hiroko is a renowned calligraphy and tea ceremony master with many students. Born in 1921, she witnessed the destruction of her home town, Tōkyō, during the Great Kantō Earthquake of 1923 and again as a result of the 1945 fire-bombing during the Great Pacific War. During the Allied Occupation after the war, she became friends with her American military neighbors. Based on this friendship, she decided to bring Americans and Japanese together through cultural exchanges, which she has continued to do with visitors from around the world.

We stayed one week at her house, which sits on a hillside above the village of Oshino-mura, with a wonderful view of Fuji-san. We slept on futons on the floor, crowded but happy. With Goto-san's smiles and quick attention to our every need, we felt like mother was at home. Brenda Wright, who had been teaching English in Tōkyō for many years, translated for us. Goto-san's longtime students came every night and cooked delicious meals for us.

One evening Goto-san brought out a small book with a delicate painting of white blossoms on the cover. It was her diary of a pilgrimage she made in 1967, walking from Kyōto to Tōkyō to pray for those who died in the war. She said she hoped some day it would be published in English. Hearing about her spiritual journey, I wanted to see her desire fulfilled.

I visited Goto-san once more, with my three sons, and she visited our family in the U.S. Between times we kept in touch. Four years passed and the idea of translating her book kept nudging me.

Early in 2005 I spent a month with Goto-san to work on what would become a dream for both of us, the English translation of her peace pilgrimage diary. The translator from my first visit, Brenda Wright, could only translate on weekends, so four Japanese volunteers took time from their busy work schedules to help. In the evenings Goto-san's son, Sumio-san, translated for his mother as we sat around the dinner table. And sometimes, when Goto-san and I were alone, huddled together with our legs under the quilt covering the heated *kotatsu* table, she would pull out an electronic translator and her huge dictionary and translate for herself.

There were challenges. Translation is a slow process, and with so many different translators, inevitably there were differences in the choice of wording, which took time to sort out. The poems were the most difficult to translate. Poetry is so subtle and the Japanese poetic language has many nuances. Fortunately, the spirit of her poems is enhanced by her beautiful *sosho*, "grass hand" calligraphy, a union of art and poetry that comes from the heart.

The process of preparing the book for publication took even longer than the translation. Just as Goto-san waited many years before she could go on pilgrimage, I also had to wait for the right time to finish the book, which for me became a kind of pilgrimage. Now it is done at last, fulfilling our wish for her story to be more widely available.

Goto-san's pilgrimage is a tender story told simply by a woman with a selfless purpose. It is also a remarkable story. There is a long tradition of pilgrimage in Japan, but Goto Hiroko may be unique as a solitary woman making such a lengthy pilgrimage. By walking slowly, with lively awareness, she experienced deep insights from nature and the people she met, which culminated for her in a spiritual awakening. I hope her story will inspire your spiritual journey.

Care Connet
March 2014

# ACKNOWLEDGMENTS

We would like to thank the translators, Brenda Wright, Watanabe Kazufumi, Joon Ou, Takahashi Hatsue, Yagi Shiomi and Goto Sumio; Kihara-shin for the paintings; and Noah Buntain and Iris Wilkinson for editing. Finally, we feel blessed with the support and love of our families throughout this project and throughout our lives.

# INTRODUCTION

My birth name is Hiroko but when I wrote this diary I used the name Suigetsu, given to me by my long-time tea ceremony master. Suigetsu means Moon Water. The moon represents truth. There is only one moon and only one truth. The water represents the heart, which is changeable, sometimes pure, sometimes not pure. The truth is so beautiful that to really see it you must look with a pure heart. The heart must be continuously cleaned because it gets dirty, like water. When you see the truth it will shine on your heart like the moon on water. The pure heart, like still clean water, will be able to reflect the truth clearly. There is a well-known Zen saying, *mizu o sukueba tsuki te ni ari*, if you scoop up water you hold the moon in your hands. The moon does not plan where it is going to reflect, it just naturally happens where the light falls. Likewise the water does not try to attract the reflection of the moon. They are both naturally there and the process of reflection just occurs naturally. In the same way the truth will naturally reflect from a pure heart.

Everyone's life is different, nobody walks the same way. Only I can walk my life. Forty-six years of my life had passed when I wrote this diary. The Great Pacific War was over. More than twenty years had gone by. After the war Japan had nothing, we had lost everything. But after twenty years we had everything, we were very rich. I cannot find anything left of the war. We have many things now but we have lost our *ki*, our spirit or life force. We live in peace in Japan now but we should not forget the war.

Many people died wishing for Japan's development and peace. Men who were conscripted into the military left their hearts with their relatives and died. Many died on Okinawa, the only place in Japan where ground fighting took place. Many more died from bomber attacks and the atomic bombs. Students with big dreams for the future had to go to war. Now we live in peace but we should not forget that many people made great sacrifices for this peace. If those people had lived they might be happy. These days many people do not know about the war. I do not want this story to be forgotten. This is the time to tell others, because I experienced the misery of war. I wrote this diary out of gratitude for my life and the spirit of the people who died in the war.

After the war I wanted to do something special to remember *senshi-sha*, the people who died in the war. Perhaps it should be a spiritual journey, a traditional pilgrimage by foot from Kyōto to Tōkyō. But this was a long, hard journey and I could not do it right away. Money, time, family, there were many obstacles, so first I made a plan. I opened the map. It was six hundred kilometers through seven prefectures. I could walk thirty kilometers in a day, so it would take twenty-five days. I decided to wait until the right time came.

I waited twenty years. My children grew up and my husband and I moved from Tōkyō to Nara. After we had been living in Nara for some time, I had a young friend, Harumi-san, who had some trouble in her home so we let her stay in our home. She knew about my plan to make a pilgrimage and one day she said, "I will take care of your family, just go ahead and do it." I was thankful and glad that the time had come.

On 6 October 1967, I started from my home, alone. I had asked that no one come to say goodbye so I left before sunrise and took the first train from Nara to Kyōto.

When I set out on foot early in the morning, I saw many white bush clover, a flower that blooms only in autumn. They were bent over with dew as if they were bowing and saying *sayōnara*.

As I said, it is six hundred kilometers from Kyōto to Tōkyō. I walked every day for twenty-five days. I do not know how I was able to walk that far but with every step I prayed for the people who died in the war. On this trip I met many people. Afterwards I felt I had become a better person. I had many valuable experiences and received many deep impressions. I could not buy that happiness with money.

清水市の聞要寺・山中徳閣住職に道を教えられる

スポーツシャツにズボン姿で
リュックを背負って颯爽？と

# Diary of the White Bush Clover

## SUIGETSU

白
萩
日
記

後
藤
水
月

# DAY 1 (6 OCTOBER)
# KYŌTO TO HAMA ŌTSU

I had a little rucksack. Inside I had underwear and clothes, a notebook, map, raincoat, toothbrush and toothpaste. That was everything.

My sneakers were new when I began to walk to Tōkyō, starting from the Kyōto Palace garden. I could hear the sound of my footsteps on the pebbles. Beside the path a puppy was in trouble. He could not jump down from the bank. I picked him up and set him down. He was glad, jumping all around. When I started walking away he followed me. I ran, the puppy ran. Maybe he is homeless, I thought, but if he is in this garden he will not have a traffic accident. I picked up the puppy and said to him, "I am starting a long journey today. I cannot take you with me so please stay here." I put him down and ran, trying to escape, but the puppy ran after me. I hid behind a tree and a building and at last he lost me. But I had lost a lot of time.

Route 1 had a lot of traffic. The air was blue with exhaust fumes. A little purple flower was blooming beside the road. I had a sudden realization that flowers do not bloom for people, they just bloom naturally. Some flowers are grown for people to look at them, like the ones in the flower shop, but little flowers growing on the side of the road, people just pass them by. However, I did notice this little wild flower so I picked one blossom and pressed it in my notebook, as if to say I admire your beauty.

After walking awhile I found a famous temple, Geshin-ji. It did not look like an *o-tera* because it was extremely small. The gate, which I opened easily, was more like the gate to a house. Nobody was around, not a sound. To my right there was a *temizuya*, a fountain with long-handled bamboo dippers, so I rinsed my face and hands and drank some water. It was cold and sweet. I thought about how travelers in ancient times must have drunk this water and refreshed their tired bodies.

At last I arrived at Hama Ōtsu in Shiga-ken, about twenty kilometers from Kyōto, my first stop. I could see Biwa-ko Bridge. It looked like a white line drawn across the lake. I headed toward Butsuryu-ji, asking someone for directions to the temple, where I had already received permission to stay. The temple was big and old, built a hundred years ago. The roof was very high, shining in the sunset.

The priest's wife came to the door smiling and said, "I thought you would be wearing white clothes because of your pilgrimage but you look very modern." I was wearing slacks, a shirt, sunglasses and a scarf.

In the evening Nitchiei-san, the priest, wrote a poem for me. The priest of Butsuryu-ji was a very scholarly man who used quite difficult *kanji*. I feel this *waka* is a comparison of the eternity of nature with the short life of a human. The temple is ancient, founded over a hundred years ago, but I stayed only one night, a very short time. My life like the autumn leaves is transitory.

*kaibyaku no*
*hiraki tamaishi*
*butsuryu-ji*
*hitoyo yadorinu*
*momijiba no aki*

At the ancient temple of Butsuryu-ji,
amongst the autumn beauty
of colorful changing leaves, I stayed one night.

佛立寺

I went to bed but the trucks on the road nearby made a lot
of noise. It was midnight yet many people were still working.

# DAY 2 (7 OCTOBER)
## HAMA ŌTSU TO MORIYAMA

Next morning at 5 o'clock the prayers began. I was in a hurry because the prayers had already started. I sat down behind the priest and prayed an hour and a half for the people who died in the war. Outside, the sunrise came. I had breakfast, gave a donation and started to walk again at 8 o'clock. From Hama Ōtsu I walked along a narrow path by the lake, where some people were enjoying fishing. I could not walk on the road because it was under construction. The old houses lining the shoreline and the narrow paths in this area reminded me of the past of Tōkaidō, the famous town road from Kyōto to Tōkyō.

I found Gichu-ji. I was happy to visit this famous temple where the ashes and bones of Kisoyoshinaka of the Genji samurai are placed. It is also well known because the poet Bashō Matusuo used to frequent the temple and write *haiku* there. To this day people who love haiku often visit that temple.

In the garden I walked around and stood in front of the stone monuments, reading the poems carved on them, which are called *hi*. I felt inspired to write two haiku.

*gichu-ji ya*
*hi ni kakomarete*
*kaki akashi*

I came to Gichu-ji –
many poems carved in rocks all around,
one deep red persimmon left on the tree.

義
仲
寺
や
碑
は
つ
ち
を
ひ
く
柿
本

The poems carved in the rocks are so old, whereas the persimmon has just grown this year. The poem contrasts the eternity of the rocks with the transience of the fruit. It is as if the persimmon wanted to show its utmost beauty before it died, this incredible deep red color. It is like humans who hope to die quickly in a moment of beauty rather than fading away in suffering and ugliness. Standing there surrounded by the stones and poems, I felt as if the persimmon were saying to me, "Look at my beauty."

*aki no hi ni*
*ura omomote naru*
*ishi no fumi*

Autumn sun on stone poems –
simple letters carved on the back,
graceful script on the face.

秋の湯にうちあそてふる石は碑

It was autumn when I came to Gichu-ji. I noticed the moss on the stones carved with hi appeared black, deep green or bright green, depending on whether the moss was in light or shadow. I was thinking about the effect of the sun striking the stone monuments and their ancient poems. The stones were not lined up in an orderly way. Some had their backs toward the sun, some faced the sun. I could feel the continuation of history of the old stones. Yet the color of the moss and the color of the stones are all different, depending on how the sunlight hits them. There is only one sun but the rays touch many stones containing many poems, with varying results.

The autumn sun striking the old poetry made me feel melancholy. The low angle of the sun in autumn has to do with change. The atmosphere of autumn is sentimental. It is a little bit of a sad season because the leaves are falling, not like spring where everything is bursting with energy. Depending on the carving on the rock face, how the light strikes it is different. On the front the poem is carved with beautiful calligraphy. On the back there are a just a few simple characters giving names and dates. Again, the sun is the same and the rock on the back and front is the same. The thing that appears different is the lettering, the contrast between the exquisite calligraphy and the plain characters.

I had a rest in front of the hut and wrote a letter. Then I started walking again. I was a little tired and had some trouble with my foot so it was hard to walk.

Beside the road there was an old cherry tree that had fallen over and the exposed roots had no soil. This *sakura* was a very old tree. I stood and looked at it with deep concentration, imagining the history of this ancient tree. The tree must have seen very noisy times with many people coming to picnic under the cherry blossoms in the spring but now there was nothing. The tree has died and the people who saw the blossoms are also nothing, all gone. Both the tree and the human beings have their span of life. Life is transient, everything has its end. We cannot win against nature so it is good to live by the grace of nature. Before I left that place I wrote a waka about what this old tree taught me.

*yowai tsuki*
*horioko sareshi*
*ro-ō no*
*hana no sakari o*
*mishi hito mo nashi*

The old cherry tree has fallen down.
Perhaps someone will dig it up.
Also the people who used to see
the beautiful blossoms –
gone.

The next town was Kusatsu Oiwake, an old border town. It must have been crowded in ancient times. There were old houses on both sides of the road. Some had been remodeled. I felt sad that the old town might change completely to the modern style in the near future. The town was noisy because of an election and there was a lot of traffic.

I was walking on the shoulder of the road next to a ditch filled with water. My feet were tired and I slipped and fell down. My leg hurt but I could not check to see how badly it was injured. In spite of the pain I continued walking toward Moriyama. People waiting for a bus were looking at me so I did not want to limp. Some part of me said, you can take a bus, but another part of me said, no, no, no, you are so chicken-hearted! I passed the bus stop and walked another ten minutes and still the bus had not come. If the people waiting for the bus had walked as I did, they would already have come as far as I had.

I had eaten breakfast in the morning but at 3 o'clock I had not had anything more to eat. There was no place to get water and few houses. I walked patiently on my painful leg. Finally I found a food shop and bought some bottles of juice. I felt like someone drinking water in the desert. The taste was delicious and different. I will never forget that taste. Afterwards I walked again feeling refreshed. By late afternoon I started wondering whether there were any *ryokan* in Moriyama. I was worried but determined. If I could not find an inn I would sleep on a bench at the station.

At 5 o'clock I saw the sign for Moriyama but I could not see any place to stay. I walked further and finally came to a big, fancy ryokan. The receptionist took one look at me and said, "This was not a place for simple travelers." I told her the purpose of my walk from Kyōto to Tōkyō. The woman said, "Wait a moment." A little while later she showed me to a special suite in a small building separate from the main ryokan. There were two rooms, very comfortable and quiet.

*Hotoke*, the Buddha's universal power, saved me. I could sleep on a bed. The *shiki-buton* underneath and *kake-buton* on top were both soft.

An attendant came, made the futon and served tea. Too much service! Then I took a look at my leg. I had a blister on my heel and a long cut on my knee. It hurt to move. I went to a pharmacy nearby, bought medicine and bandages, and dressed the wound.

I had been walking all day, more than twenty kilometers, and I was really tired. When I could finally rest in the ryokan I looked out the window and suddenly the rain started. If it had rained while I was walking I would not have felt that wonderful feeling of the sound of rain, *potsu-potsu*, because I would have been getting all wet. I felt incredibly relieved and happy that I had made it there before the rain. Because I could sit back and rest, the sound of the rain was magical.

Dinner was gorgeous and delicious and I was thankful for the meal. I made a haiku and spoke it aloud while the attendant was serving my meal.

*moriyama ni*
*tsuku ya shigure no*
*yado no mado*

Finally arriving at Moriyama,
resting in a small room –
autumn rain outside the window.

The serving woman asked for a copy, so I wrote it down and gave it to her. I tried to sleep because I had to walk again tomorrow. But then I heard someone say, *"Sumimasen."* It was the same woman, bringing *ryoshi* paper. "Excuse me," she said again. "The owner wants a copy of the haiku too." So I wrote the haiku on that special calligraphy paper with love and gratitude.

I was awakened by sounds from next door. Alarmed, I opened the sliding *fusuma* and looked out. Through the open fusuma of the next house I saw an old woman cleaning up the kitchen and an old man who appeared to be sick, sitting on the bed. Seeing that everything was all right I closed my fusuma and went back to bed, but I lay awake thinking about the old couple. I wondered if they were the owner's parents. The owners were making noise with the wealthy guests while the two old people were living in simple circumstances and perhaps sickness. There was such a contrast between the two lifestyles. The impression of the old woman taking care of her husband stayed with me for a long time.

# DAY 3 (8 OCTOBER)
# MORIYAMA TO OMIHACHIMAN

I had already paid the ryokan fee, so before the attendants woke I started to walk again. All along the way I kept looking at the triangular shape of one big mountain. In this area the surrounding mountains were low but this mountain stood out, shaped like a mountain made of sand. I liked this mountain. From some places it appeared to be one mountain but in fact there were three peaks, so it was called Mikami-yama, Three Spirits Mountain. I walked along the busy road, looking at these peaks in the clear morning air.

I was hungry because I started without breakfast. In a small shop I drank a bottle of milk. I just stood because when I sat I felt pain in my knee.

Walking on I found a very nice house on the right with a low stone wall. The stone was very old and every stone had a groove running straight across the face. I touched the groove. I could tell it was not carved by anyone but it looked like a design. I asked an old man working beside me, "Is this stone made of lodestone?" It looked like the lines made in old times by iron wheels on the stone pavement. This line is wonderful, I thought, it's very interesting. The design is very smooth, not sharp. It could not have been made by human hands. This house has precious treasures.

Afterwards I walked and walked but there were no houses. I wanted to ask someone about a ryokan for the night but there was no one around. Someone had told me I could find places to stay if I went to the train station so I hurried there. As far as I could see there were only rice fields, golden colored, the heads bending down. The time was near sunset. The sun would go down soon so I was worried and hurried on.

As I walked through the golden rice fields a mendicant monk came toward me from the opposite direction. He was powerfully built and walked with long strides. He was wearing a *kasa*, a wide domed wheat straw hat worn by pilgrims, and black *koromo*, the robes flapping in the wind. When we passed I caught a glimpse of his bearded face under his kasa. It was an extremely stern face, but just in the moment we passed we both smiled a little. We bowed to each other. We moved on and the distance separating us grew and grew. I walked to the east, he walked to the west. We did not know each other but at that moment I felt a very warm Buddhist teaching. That one tiny point in time was magnificent. I thought of the saying, *ichi go ichi e* – one time, one meeting.

*aki ōmi*
*tabi yuku so to*
*emi kawashi*

Autumn in Ōmi –
crossing paths with a wandering monk,
exchanging little smiles.

秋近江
たふゆく
僧と笑
ゝ麦し

After that I arrived at the station. I asked, "Are there any ryokan around here?" They told me the location of one. Standing in front of it I wondered if I should stay there. The sign on the house said it was a ryokan but it looked rather decrepit. I decided I would not stay there. I went back to the station to check the telephone book for another inn. I found one, a youth hostel, and called. They said, *"Ōkē."* But I was surprised to hear where this *yūsu-hosuteru* was, twelve kilometers away. I thought it was impossible to walk there this late so I apologized to Buddha and took a bus.

When I got there I found that the hostel was built halfway up the mountain and you had to walk up. As I started climbing up, an old lady in a shop called to me. She said, "You'll need a walking stick but you don't need to rent it. I'll give this *tsue* to you for free." Even though the road to the hostel was very steep I thought I did not need a walking stick, I could climb by myself, but I accepted her offer. Bending forward I climbed step by step, clasping the walking stick behind my back.

At last I reached the hostel and gave thanks for the day's trip. I had already walked three days but I still had not walked half way around Biwa-ko and the lake seemed as big as the sea. I felt really tired. I took a bath, massaged my legs and put menthol plasters on all the sore spots on my body. My daughter had put the *shippu* in my bag and now I really appreciated her thoughtfulness. I went to bed still sore. It was hard to write in my notebook but I knew I would forget if I did not. Sitting beside the window I wrote a letter and an entry in my diary.

I could see the moon reflected on the lake and the lights of Ōtsu Bridge. I had seen these lights for the past two nights. I really liked this bridge and I got a little nostalgic when I realized I would not see it again as I journeyed on. Because I had been walking slowly on my pilgrimage, the impressions of the lights on the bridge went much deeper in my heart. Thinking of Ōtsu Bridge, I went to bed.

# DAY 4 (9 OCTOBER)
# OMIHACHIMAN TO HIKONE

I woke up to the sound of motor boats. Nowadays no one rows a boat to catch fish. My body felt sore and it was hard to wake up. I washed my face. Looking out the window I could see morning dew covering the beautiful mountainside. With affection I bid farewell to Biwa-ko. I left the hostel, remembering to take the walking stick. I climbed further up to Chomei-ji and prayed to Kannon-sama. Then I started down the stone steps in front of the temple. It was very steep. I noticed that each step had a round hole for the tip of a tsue. It is like the ups and downs in life, I thought. When things are going well you do not feel you need help. But when things go wrong, you must slow down and realize that you need to draw upon the support of your inner strength.

Using the walking stick I went down more than five hundred steps. I gave the tsue back to the woman at the shop with a contribution of 100 yen for her kindness. I said, "Thank you. I learned a wonderful lesson from this walking stick." The bus came and I started to get on but the woman came up to me carrying a package of chopsticks. She said, "These special *hashi* are to wish you long life. Please use them." Once more I thanked her. This woman did not want to sell the chopsticks and I did not want to buy them because they were an expression of gratitude between us. I felt very warm inside my heart.

At the end of the bus ride I got off and walked again. There was little traffic in this area because it was far away from the busy road. It looked like an old road. I asked people and they said, yes, it was. The houses were built far apart and the village was quiet. The grass was already withered. I could hear the sound of insects even in the afternoon. Then I walked again. My leg was in better condition now because it had warmed up from the morning's walk. I had to reach Hikone by evening. It was the longest distance I traveled on this journey. I walked along eating sweets, looking down at my feet and not at the distance I had to go.

Later I walked past a hill. I could see golden rice fields all around and people busily working in the fields with machines. Many years ago rice was harvested by hand. Now the machines were convenient but very expensive. The farmers were working hard and may have seen me only as a hiker with a rucksack. I felt sorry because I was not working hard like them. However, in my own way I was doing hard work because I was on a pilgrimage.

A little girl sat on the side of the road. She looked bored. Maybe she was waiting until her parents finished working. An old woman and a girl were working a small area by hand. The woman was very old but she was doing this work usually done by young people. If only I had time I would help them. I went over and spoke to the old woman. She told me, "My son died in the war but the field is still here so I have to reap the rice."

"I am walking to pray for the people who died in the war," I said, "so please tell me your son's name and I will pray for him tonight at the temple where I will be staying." She gave me his name and thanked me. It was past noon so I had to hurry. This was the first and the last time I would meet this old woman. I said to her, "Please take care and live long." After a few minutes I looked back and saw the old woman and the girl waving.

*banshu ya*
*robā no tenaru*
*inaho kana*

End of autumn –
old woman carrying in her arms
sheaves of cut rice.

I had to hurry to Hikone but I got lost because I did not look at the map. There were no shops but I found a few people who were buying fruit and vegetables in front of a farmer's house. I bought three bananas and asked them how to find the road to Hikone. It was twenty kilometers to Hikone and it was already 2 o'clock. I wondered if I could make it before dark and how long I could walk.

Eventually I found the railroad track and a train station. I wondered if it was Hikone, but no, it was one station before. Until I found the train line I had great energy but when I realized I had to walk more I felt weak. I walked slowly. The sun was setting. There was no bus. I had to go by foot. I walked beside that railroad track for four kilometers.

Finally I arrived at Hikone but I had to walk all the way through the town to the temple. I wanted to cry. I called ahead to say I would arrive that night. The priest at Choei-ji said, "Oh, you're really coming?" It was so late, he was wondering if I would come or not.

An hour later I reached the temple at last. I could not speak but only said to Buddha, "I have arrived." I ate supper and gave thanks for it. I really enjoyed taking a bath. Today's trip was long and I had lost my way. That day was the longest and fullest day of my entire trip. I felt so thankful for the day's events and a comfortable end to the day.

I got a call from my family. Their voices were very kind. My daughter said, "Take it easy, you can come back anytime."

"It is all right, I am going on," I replied.

Afterwards I talked about my journey with the priest and his wife. After spending a few days by myself I missed people very much. I felt as if I had been walking in the desert, so when I met one person I felt happy.

# DAY 5 (10 OCTOBER)
# HIKONE TO SEKIGAHARA

After breakfast the priest's wife made me a lunch of bread, milk and fruit. My rucksack was full. It was heavy but I thanked them. Saying farewell to the priest's family I walked to Road Number 8. Soon I entered a tunnel. There were no lights, it was very dark. Cars made loud noises passing by me. Lights shone on me. Whenever a car passed I turned my face to the wall. If a driver happened to see me in my black coat he must have thought I looked like a bat clinging to the wall! After a little while I could hardly breathe in the tunnel because of the fumes.

Passing Maibara, there were two ways to go. The left went to Hokuriku area, the right went to Nakasendo. I chose the right. Cars mostly went to the left so I relaxed while I walked, humming a song. I wanted to take a rest so I looked at my watch. An hour had already passed and I had walked four kilometers. I sat down on the bank and ate some lemon drops. School children came toward me in a line. It was a very Japanese picture: thatch roofs, bamboo forest and golden rice fields. After ten minutes I stood up and stretched my muscles. They felt sore but I could stand all right.

I met a student walking with his bicycle. He must have thought I was a young girl, wearing sunglasses, pants and a scarf. He stopped to talk with me.

"I am walking to Tōkyō," I told him.

He was surprised and asked, "How old are you?"

"How old do you think I am?"

"Twenty years old."

It was noon, not night time! We say, *yome, toume, kasa no uchi, no kao wa wakaranai* – seen in the evening, seen from far away, inside the umbrella, you do not know the face. I thought perhaps the sunglasses made me look young but even so his compliment made me happy. We said sayōnara, wishing health and success to each other. He said he had started from his house early in the morning and was going to Kyōto. The boy went off to the west and I went off to the east.

After walking for a while I found the old original road, the Nakasendo, and next to it was the modern road with cars, running parallel to each other. I started walking on the Nakasendo. No cars were allowed on the old road, which was made of large stones, bumpy now after so many centuries. The gardens of the houses that lined this road had been kept in good condition. Right in front of me I could see a small mountain but I felt it had a lot of power. However, the side of the mountain had been scraped bare, as it was being quarried for sand to make cement. It was very painful to see this, a great shame to see such a beautiful mountain being destroyed by human greed.

I walked slowly until I arrived at a small village where I had planned to stay but there was no inn. I asked a villager and he said I would find accommodations in a place called Sekigahara, four kilometers away. On the right hand side of the road in front of a house there was a ceramic statue of Fukusuke, a fat, happy bringer of good fortune with long ears. The statue was smiling at me as I walked by.

I came to a very old, weathered sign for a pharmacy, which had been there for hundreds of years. When I looked into the store it was filled with old furniture, desks and chairs, which had darkened with age. The owner of the store came out, a very elegant old lady. She asked where I had come from. I explained that I still had to walk ten days more. The lady went into the back of the store and brought out some medicine and gave it to me. She said, "This is a special medicine made only by my family for our family." She said I would need it on my travels. It was good for anything. Usually they did not sell this to customers. The lady showed me a woodblock print of this pharmacy by Hiroshige Andō, the famous nineteenth-century *ukiyo-e* artist, especially known for *The Fifty-three Stations of the Tōkaidō*. That smiling statue of Fukusuke was in the print. As I left she said, "Please come again."

After walking for half an hour I stopped at a place where there had once been a checkpoint for crossing the border. In the past there used to be barrier gates between the prefectures. Stern-looking officials would stop people to check their personal documents and try to intercept bad people. They do not have these checkpoints anymore but something remains – old buildings, posts. I had started from Kyōto and traveled a long way, finally arriving at this old border station. In the past I would have had to present all my papers to get through but now there was nobody there and I could freely and easily cross the border. A long time ago it used to be a busy place because people wanted to hurry through. But now the only thing left was a stone monument and it was very peaceful. Later I wrote this waka:

*kyo yori no*
*tabiji haruka ni*
*ayumi kite*
*ima seki koyuru*
*fuwa no yamazato*

Walking all the way from Kyōto,
crossing the old border station at Fuwa,
now completely quiet.

京より
旅路
の
はて
今
まで

不破の山里

After walking a while I reached Sekigahara station, where
I found a place to stay, the Sekigahara Hotel, a very big *hoteru*.
I took a taxi from the station to the hotel. The owner of the

hotel paid for my taxi because he knew why I was walking. The owner and his wife were very kind. After dinner they joined me in my room and we had a conversation about this area, which is the site of a famous climactic battle during the feudal period in Japan. The owner told me that many samurai died in this area. After the battle the people gathered the remains of the unidentified warriors and made a memorial to the dead. Later they made a little theme park next to the hotel, called War Land Park, with a small replica of the battle. Soon after the war monument was built, the owner of the hotel erected a statue of Kannon-sama in the park.

This was the kind of conversation we had, about life being precious and that we should use it wisely. Dew is quickly evaporated by the morning sun. Our lifetime is as momentary as the dew. Because our life is so transient we must realize its importance. Before we die we must try to do as many good things as possible to validate our lives. Let us not die in futility, wasting our lives. We talked this way until sunrise. Afterwards I wrote a waka about our conversation.

*kimi mo ware mo*
*tsuyu no inochi o*
*oshimu nari*
*ada ni shiseji to*
*katari akashitsu*

Both you and me,
our lifetimes are as momentary as the dew.
Recognize that life is precious,
do not waste it.
We talked this way until sunrise.

惜しからぬ
命を捨てて
あたなる
あたき死
と
誘ひあひに
けり

# DAY 6 (11 OCTOBER)
# SEKIGAHARA TO ŌGAKI

In the morning I went to pray at the statue of Kannon-sama. When I left I realized I did not have to pay for my room. The owner allowed me to stay for free and also paid for my breakfast.

I began walking again. After awhile I stopped at a store and used the telephone to call the temple where I was planning to stay that night because I knew the priest would be worried. I told him I was fine, I was walking well. The owner of the store overheard me mentioning the reason for my walk. She began to cry because she lost her younger brother in the war and she had not thought about him in a long time. The store owner said that even though she had forgotten about her brother a long time ago, someone she did not know could walk and pray for her brother. She was very moved by that. The woman gave me some milk and some money. I asked for her younger brother's name and told the woman I would use the money at the next temple to pray for him. I wrote his name in my notebook and left.

While I was walking I passed a milestone that was placed there by Tokugawa Ieyasu, who became the first shogun of Japan in 1600. I thought abut the Tokugawa family, who ruled until 1867 when the shogunate was overthrown and the newly enthroned emperor began the Meiji reign. The Edo period under the Tokugawa was a long era of peace marked by sakoku, national seclusion. Some of my ancestors were connected with the Tokugawa.

Soon I arrived at Ōgaki, a river port with docks for small boats. Ōgaki was the last place the *haikai* poet Bashō stopped before he took a boat back home at the end of his travels all around Japan. I felt glad to visit the small historical park at Ōgaki with a memorial monument dedicated to Bashō, who lived from 1644 to 1694. Some of his poems were carved on stones and both the stones and the monument were lit up. As I walked around reading the poems, I reflected on Bashō's travels.

Close to that park was the temple where I planned to stay. The head priest came to welcome me with a smile. When he saw me he said, "Oh, Goto-san, you are in *jakko*." I was surprised to hear him say I was in heaven because I was not dead. He explained that there are two kinds of paradise. One is where you go when you die and the other is heaven on earth. You can still be in heaven while you are alive if you are surrounded by *satori*, peace and contentment. Because I was walking for peace, not making any money for myself, it was like I was already in paradise. I learned something new from the priest because I did not know about the two kinds of heaven. The priest apologized that the temple was too small for anyone to stay in, so he had arranged for me to stay in a local ryokan, which he paid for.

# DAY 7 (12 OCTOBER)
## ŌKAGI TO ICHINOMIYA

At 5 o'clock in the morning I went back to the temple for a one-hour prayer session with the priest. Then I began walking once again. I had to cross bridges over three big rivers, Ibi-gawa, Nagara-gawa and Kiso-gawa. After walking nineteen kilometers I took a break. A bullet train passed right beside me, startling me. I wanted to compare my pace with the *shinkansen* and I calculated that one day of my walking was equivalent to ten minutes on the train. It might be the same distance but the meaning was completely different. I was very happy to be walking and praying.

When I reached Nagara-gawa I saw that there was a special pedestrian path along the side of the bridge. Usually I had to hurry across a bridge because it was only for cars. I stopped in the middle of this bridge and looked at the river. The water was very low and I realized it was because there was a dam upstream.

Nagara-gawa is famous for *ukai*, fishing with trained cormorants, big water birds that catch fish by scooping them up in their large beaks. The fishermen capture the birds and put them on a tether with a band around their neck so that they cannot swallow the fish they catch. I looked at the river and wondered whether right now someone was making the birds catch fish and then stealing the fish to eat for themselves. I stood there reflecting on that as I looked down at the water.

After crossing the river I arrived at Ichinomiya. I was hungry so I went to a crowded *soba* shop. I had not spoken to anybody the whole day. When I went into the noodle shop I felt as if I was stepping into a completely different world because it was so noisy and crowded.

Ichinomiya is famous for textiles and I could hear the sound of the looms as I walked through the streets. At last I arrived at the temple. The priest there had the same family name as myself, Goto. When I first saw his face he appeared a bit scary but after talking to him he appeared to be very interesting and kind.

As soon as I arrived at the temple the priest asked me if I would like to go to a temple in Gifu with him, which was about ten kilometers away. He asked in this way, "I am going to Gifu, what do you want to do?" I thought he was testing me. I could have said I was tired and taken a rest but if I did not go I might lose the opportunity to visit another temple. The priest walked without considering how tired I was and that I had been walking all day. From the temple we walked to the station. The steps were steep and I was so tired I felt like crying. I was really hungry and felt freezing cold in the wind. Also my hair was all a mess. I believed all this was a trial for me. When I arrived at the temple in Gifu I was revived by a big bowl full of white rice and felt a bit livelier after eating. We got back to Ichinomiya around 10 o'clock. I was so tired I just fell into bed.

# DAY 8 (13 OCTOBER)
# ICHINOMIYA TO NAGOYA

Today I planned to arrive in Nagoya. It has been a week since I left my home. Thanks to Harumi-san, who is looking after my children, I am free now because of you, I thought, and my family also helped me very much. I hope they are not too inconvenienced by my absence. Saigyō, a samurai who became a monk, left his home to walk with the Buddha. He became a famous master of *tanka* poetry but he also thought of his family as he was walking.

I concentrated on walking east but thoughts of my family still came to mind. I looked down at my feet, walking step by step. Suddenly I heard the noise of the city. Looking up I found that I was already in the city. The smog looked like dust in the air. I had been walking in the countryside so I hated the noise and polluted air.

At noon I arrived at Nagoya Castle. Walking on the pebbled path made the soles of my feet hurt. I had walked four hours without any rest. I took a break in a small shop where I bought milk and bread and ate them. The girl who worked in the shop had a sharp tongue and some of the customers seemed timid and nervous. Her hair and makeup were done nicely but she was not kind. Looking at the situation for a while, I could see that it was due to the attitude of the supervisor, who was also not kind. The *sempai* should have trained the workers with her heart.

I sat in the park and wrote letters to everybody. Then I began walking again but I misread the map and walked away from the temple by mistake. The town looked like Tōkyō, with many shops selling clothes and goods. I did not want to look at them at all. I just felt as if I were wearing the black robes of a monk.

At last I arrived at Kenkoku-ji. The temple had been rebuilt recently and looked like a modern building. I thought it must have been a great undertaking of labor and finances for the people connected with this temple. The priest and his wife were very kind, warm people. Before I left on my journey I had received an express letter from them saying it was all right to stay at the temple, so I already felt their kindness. I prayed in the temple and then the wife made dinner for me and served it in a special room usually used only by the head priest. I was deeply grateful because I felt perhaps I was not worthy of such an honor. But they allowed me to use this special room so I gave thanks to Buddha.

After dinner I took my notebook to the priest and asked him to put it on the altar in the temple, as I always did. The notebook contained the names and dates of the people I knew who had died in the war as well as my purpose to include everyone who had died. The priest explained about the temple's *honzon*, the principle image, and prayed over my notebook.

# DAY 9 (14 OCTOBER)
# NAGOYA TO OKAZAKI

Today was a special day, the anniversary of the death of the previous head priest. The praying started at 5 o'clock in the morning. Putting on my clothes, I hurried to the main room of the temple. Many believers came to pray. The current head priest explained to the worshippers why I was there, so they also prayed over my notebook.

At 8 o'clock the priest's wife saw me off. I walked a different way, off the old Tōkaidō. This road was very wide with a lot of traffic in Nagoya. It was hard to walk because the road was built for cars, not pedestrians.

Then I saw a *hana densha*, a small train with only one carriage, covered with fresh flowers and all lit up. It was specially decorated as part of a city festival. There were many decorated dolls inside the carriage. Many people with children lined both sides of the street to watch the train pass. When I was a child I had seen the flower train during the *matsuri* in Tōkyō every year. At that time the dolls were Momotarō, the super boy born of a peach, and Hanasaka Jiijii, the old man who made withered cherry trees blossom, and also Kaguya-hime, the princess of the moon. But the dolls in this train were Atom Boy and monsters!

Leaving Nagoya I felt freed from the pollution and noise of traffic. I visited Honyo-ji, a very small temple on the edge of the city. I had only heard about it the day before from the priest at Kenkoku-ji so I did not have an appointment. An old woman, the wife of the priest of Honyo-ji, came towards me and I spoke with her about my journey.

The priest prayed over my notebook. We talked together, sitting around the warm fire of the hibachi. The priest and his wife were always smiling and I felt their warmth in my heart. I felt lucky that I happened to go there because they could truly understand the meaning of my journey. In my travels I had met many people and felt many things. Most people cannot usually understand each other's deep feelings just by talking and listening but these people could.

This temple was not big or fancy but there I felt so much peace. I recalled the words of the priest at Ōgaki about the two kinds of heaven. Now I understood what he had meant by satori. I also felt I came to understand the heart of *sadō*, the way of tea, which means serving from the heart. After meeting the priest and his wife at Honyo-ji, I felt they exemplified the essence of sadō. Before I left, the priest prayed for my safety on my travels. He also wrote a poem for me.

*myoho no*
*ontomo o shite*
*jyakko e*
*sankei sen no*
*keiko naramashi*

Walking humbly with the power of nature
to arrive at enlightenment
is one kind of spiritual practice,
is it not?

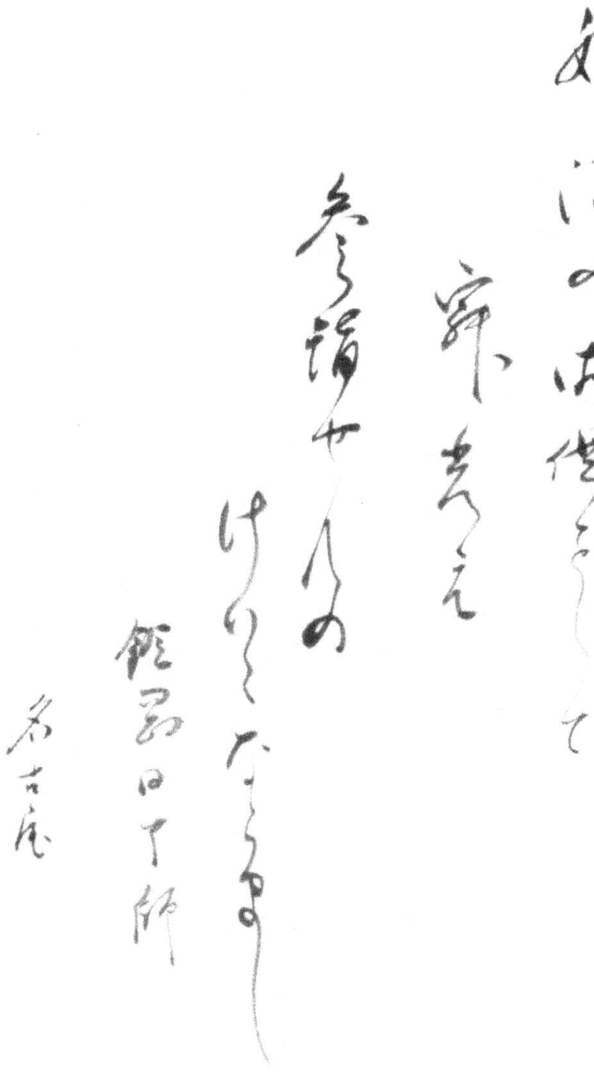

One way to attain enlightenment is by sitting to meditate. The priest was saying that I was also practicing meditation by walking.

When the sun began to set, I crossed over the Yahagi Bridge. This was the historic place where the famous samurai leaders, Toyotomi Hideyoshi and Hachisuka Koroku, were destined to meet for the first time. Toyotomi Hideyoshi was living there when he met Hachisuka Koroku and thereafter Hideyoshi became a famous *daimyō*. He is referred to by his first name because it was traditional to use the first name of top leaders to avoid confusion since they usually had the same family name. As I crossed the bridge I thought again about the wonder of human destiny. I arrived at the home of the Abe family just as the lights of the houses were being turned on.

# DAY 10 (15 OCTOBER)
# OKAZAKI TO GAMAGORI

Last night I enjoyed talking with the Abe family until 1 o'clock in the morning. After a short night of sleep, they came with me to the sub-temple of Kenkoku-ji to pray over the notebook.

At 8 o'clock I started walking along Route 247. After a little while it became a country road. Running beside the road was the Tōkaidō railway. In some of the train carriages I could see school children on an excursion. They waved at me as the trains passed going west and east. I remembered when I was a school girl going on field trips by train many, many years ago. I also had talked with my friends and waved to people on the road.

While I walked I ate rice balls wrapped in seaweed. It was not good manners to eat *onigiri* and walk but I did not have much time. It was a very simple road. I walked for six hours, step by step. Sometimes I stopped to look at the map to make sure of where I was. The map was completely *boro-boro* after being opened and closed so many times. I repaired it with many pieces of cellophane tape.

At last I could see the sea. I had not seen it for a long time. The sun was setting against the horizon and the silver waves were shining, *pika-pika*. I arrived at a city. On my right side I could see Takeshima, an island that held a special honzon of Benten-sama, the Shinto water goddess. Today was the

Benten festival and many stalls had been set up. I took a boat to Takeshima to pray to Benten-sama and came back to the mainland.

Finally I reached Takeshima Hotel. My room had an ocean view. The sea breeze softly brushed my cheek. I saw someone fishing. Everywhere the sky and the sea were turning red in the sunset. I took a bath and then went for a walk along the seashore. It was hard to walk on the sand and my legs were very tired, but after soaking in the hot water of the *o-furo* I needed to stretch my legs. The fish I had for dinner was delicious. After dinner I wrote in my diary.

The son of the hotel owner came into my room and I talked with him about my diary. "You walked from Kyōto?" he asked, surprised. I said, "Please do not forget the many people who lost their lives in the war." He was a young man but he cried listening to my story. Nowadays many young people say, "Why didn't they refuse to go to the war?" Or they say, "It's nonsense to die for one's country." But this young boy had a gentle, pure mind, so he could understand. I try not to push my ideas on young people. I just talk to them and some day they may understand the real meaning of the preciousness of life.

# DAY 11 (16 OCTOBER)
# GAMAGORI TO TOYOHASHI

While the people in the hotel were still sleeping, I went out for a walk by the sea. It was very calm and I breathed deeply. Far away I saw fishing boats coming back to shore. I thought I had gotten up early but I realized that someone had risen even earlier and had already finished their work for the day.

Today I walked to Toyohashi, arriving a day earlier than I had originally planned. On the way, I stood at the bottom of a hill and prayed to the statue of Kōbō-Daishi, which stood at the top of the hill. Kūkai, known after death as Kōbō-Daishi, brought the teachings of Buddhism back from China. He studied at Heian temple in Kyōto and then went on to found the tantric Shingon sect and Kōyasan, a mountain retreat. The statue faced Mikawa Bay and the far horizon. Traveling by shinkansen you could only see the back of the statue but on my walk I was able to see his face.

I worried about the amount of traffic. In the distant past the road was originally built for people walking, but now the emphasis was on the importance of cars, and pedestrians are forced to walk on the side of the road. It is especially dangerous for old people and children. It is a pity. Three men offered me a ride. One was a young truck driver, one was a middle-aged businessman and one was an older man. Thanking each of them, I refused and continued walking.

I wanted to post my letters in the town of Maeshiba, so I entered the post office beside the road. As soon as I opened the door, three young women working in the post office said *"Konichiwa"* in unison. I was surprised and looked around but I was the only customer there. I said "Good afternoon" in return to them. I could not believe that all three of them would greet one person. Usually officials have a reputation of not being so polite. If all public officials were like these women, people would feel more at ease.

I entered Toyohashi without having had anything to eat from morning until 1:30 in the afternoon. I could walk all day without eating. People can work without food for one or two days. I had lunch at a roadside restaurant. Next door was a service station. I asked for a memento stamp for my diary. Two men working in greasy clothes were surprised to see my notebook. "Good luck on your journey and take care," they said and waved goodbye. I telephoned the next temple. I thought perhaps it was nearby but it was on the other side of the town, so I felt disappointed and tired. If I rested I would arrive too late, so I started walking with determination.

After awhile I reached the suburb on the outskirts of Toyohashi and found the temple. The priest of the sub-temple of Honmyo-ji welcomed me warmly. The priest's mother was *ama-san*, a Buddhist nun. She said to me, "Let's go to the *sentō* together. You need to relax and refresh yourself after your hard walk." It had been a long time since I had been to a public bath. In the bath I looked around at the many women, all strangers to me. But everybody was naked together in the bath and some were talking to each other. It is a very special Japanese way. I had never thought about the sentō in this way before. Without saying anything we could trust each other and feel connected. That night I slept easily, feeling completely at home.

# DAY 12 (17 OCTOBER)
# TOYOHASHI TO NAGASHINO
# AND BACK TO TOYOHASHI

Since I had arrived at Toyohashi one day earlier than expected, I decided to stay one more night there. In the morning I asked the priest to pray for my notebook and in the afternoon we took a train together to Nagashino, the site of the famous battle between Takeda Shingen and Tokugawa Ieyasu. Takeda was a samurai from Kai, now called Yamanashi-ken. Kyōto was the capital city at that time and every samurai wanted to control Kyōto. Takeda tried to go to Kyōto, but on the way, Tokugawa, who ruled Mikawa, now called Aichi-ken, fought Takeda and his men at Mikatagahara. Takeda won this battle but he died soon afterwards, and Tokugawa eventually became the shogun of all Japan.

On the edge of the small town of Nagashino was a mountain, called Horai-san, famous for its many *bupposo*, a kind of owl. It rained a little and I realized it had been quite a while since it had rained. It was a little bit cold.

We arrived at the house where the priest was taking me. There was a pub in front. The priest went straight through the pub and entered the house without any introduction. In front of the family altar he lit a candle and some incense and began to pray. The owner was not there so I thought it was strange. The owner was in the pub, singing with the customers very loudly and clapping. I was very surprised. The priest continued praying. I was angry because the priest was a good man, praying at the family altar, but instead of the family joining him, the owner was singing in the pub.

Later on a young woman came in with a donation for the priest. I looked at her face. She was one of the singers in the pub. The priest's face was smiling as he talked to her but I was not smiling at all. She served the priest some *sakē*. She was drunk and could not speak properly but their conversation became very serious. She had hated her parents because they did not believe in her. They had treated her differently than her brothers so she left home. At first she worked as a waitress but gradually her life got worse and she fell into the wrong kind of work, but nobody noticed. She tried again to work in a restaurant but if they knew about her past they did not want to employ her.

The owner of this pub knew all about her past but gave her a job anyway. So she worked hard for this woman because the pub owner had helped her through a difficult time. There were tears in her eyes as she said, "I want to marry and be a wife and have children." She did not look like the drunken woman I had seen a moment ago. I felt ashamed of myself. Now I looked at her through rose-colored glasses. I had only seen her from the surface, not her inner self. She was just like a flower blooming from the mud. Her body had been violated but her heart was pure. The way she acted in front of the customers was just part of her job. I was touched by this woman. The priest had known everything about her. Later that evening when we got on the train she came to see us off. She looked like a different woman. Her manner was extremely polite as she said sayōnara to us. Listening to the sound of the rain, I reflected on what had happened that evening.

# DAY 13 (18 OCTOBER)
# TOYOHASHI TO KANZAN-JI

After praying over my notebook, the priest, his wife and his mother came to the temple gate to see me off. The priest's mother was a nun. Ama-san gave me a *mawata*, a fluffy square silk cloth to drape across one's back to keep warm. She said, "You will feel cold when you cross over Hakone-yama. This is very light and compact." She looked like my grandmother so I was very glad and thankful for her gift.

It would take me ten days to get to Hakone-yama. Hakone is not one mountain but a ring of mountains, the remains of a volcanic caldera, with a big lake called Hamana-ko in the center. It would take me three to four hours to climb over Tametoge, the high pass on the west side of the caldera.

After I cross over the Tametoge, I thought, I will be in Shizuoka-ken. The road to Tametoge was wet from the rain the previous night. The mountain air was fresh and clear and I thought it was a good atmosphere for contemplation. However, there were many dead frogs and snakes on the road. Frogs like water and must have been happy that the rain was pouring after a long time so they jumped, *pyon-pyon*, onto the rain-filled road, but the cars came and crushed them. I felt sorry for them. If they had remained croaking in the rice field they would have been safe. I suddenly remembered the battle place. Humans and frogs are different but when I saw the dead frogs I thought, humans die just like that on the battlefield, do they not? They were not killed by cars but by more terrible weapons. I stopped and prayed for the people who died in battle, and for the frogs.

There was a toll gate for cars to cross the first mountain in the Hakone range so I asked whether there was a fee for pedestrians.

The official asked, "Are you walking from here?"

"Yes, I already walked here, so I will continue walking."

"From where?"

"From Kyōto."

"That's amazing!"

He did not charge me anything. Perhaps I am the only person in the world who ever walked from the toll gate over the Tametoge to Hamana-ko. The mountain road had many curves. On one side I saw a river in the valley below, on the other side was the steep mountain. The fragrance of the trees after the rain wafted on the air. When I was a student, the teacher used to sing the song of Hakone and now I sang this song to help me walk. A few days later, I thought, I will cross over Hakone-yama. Today is just a trial. I could see the toll gate looking very small far below. I had already climbed to a high elevation and I was thankful for my two legs. There were many big red rocks on the mountainside so this first mountain was called Akaiwa-yama, Red Rock Mountain.

At last I arrived at the entrance to the tunnel between the prefectures. I could see Toyohashi below. I had stayed two days in that city and had met people there so I turned back to wave to them. Sayōnara Toyohashi, I will miss you. Then I entered the tunnel. There were no lights. It was so dark I could not see the end of the tunnel. After walking two hundred meters, I came out on the other side.

I had now entered Shizuoka-ken. Suddenly I could see Hamana-ko clearly below, as if I could reach out and touch the lake. The north end had many inlets. I walked down the steep slope, going so fast I was almost running. On both sides there were *mikan* orchards with thousands of golden tangerines. If I stretched out my hand, I could easily pick them, but I could not do that because I was on a pilgrimage. The pickups passing me on the road were on their way to spray the orchards. I will remember this scene the next time I eat a tangerine. Since breakfast I had not had any food and now it was 2 o'clock but there were no food shops around. Feeling hungry, I hiked down the mountain.

When I arrived at Mikkabi, famous for mikan, I saw signs advertising orchards where you could pick your own tangerines. I walked up and down and around all the inlets. My legs were a little sore. At last the road became flat. I was walking along the original road. Beside it the new Tomei Expressway was under construction. The rain last night had washed the dust from the road. This road would be noisy after the expressway was finished and we would never be able to experience this calmness again.

I wanted to go to Kanzan-ji, a temple on the south side of the lake. I would either have to walk all the way around or take a boat across. To walk would take a long time so I decided to go in a small motorboat. At the dock I saw a sign, "Please hang this flag." If the flag was hanging, the boat would take passengers for free. The wind on the lake was a little cold as it was already the middle of October.

# DAY 14 (19 OCTOBER)
## KANZAN-JI TO HAMAMATSU

At Kanzan-ji I shared a room with three women. After breakfast in the temple we wished each other a safe trip and I started out at 8 o'clock. I already had a reservation for the *shukubō*, the temple lodgings where I would stay that night. I felt relaxed because I did not have to worry about finding a place.

In the fields I passed there were many chrysanthemums, carefully supported with stakes. The *kiku* blossoms were big and beautiful. In the corner of the field many small flowers had been thrown away but they were also blooming. Nature had given life to them equally but those kiku discarded in the corner were entirely different. Unlike the flowers that had been looked after carefully, these rejected flowers were weak and had grown crookedly. I felt that those flowers taught me about the human condition. I stood in front of them and contemplated their message for a little while.

I walked three hours from Kanzan-ji around Hamanaka-ko. They were constructing a bridge over the lake. In the future we would be able to cross the lake without taking a boat. After checking the map I walked into Hamamatsu. The airplanes of the Self Defense Forces were training in the blue sky. My cousin who died during the war had also taken this training and became a *kamikaze* pilot. I looked at the sky and the airplanes, wishing we had never had a war and that young people had never died like that.

Passing Komaki town I walked beside a castle. I asked directions to Yogyo-ji and found the temple easily. It was not big but looked old. A priest and his son looked after the temple. I had a little free time so I went to Hamamatsu train station where I bought some sweets and pickles and sent them home. I had not remembered for a long time that I was a housewife. My face was tanned from so much sun.

I ate dinner with the priest's family. The priest talked about his two grandsons with a smile. He was both a priest and an ordinary grandfather. Today had been an eventful day.

# DAY 15 (20 OCTOBER) HAMAMATSU TO OSUGACHU

At half past 5 o'clock in the morning the prayers had already started in the main room of the temple. The priest and his son said prayers for the people whose names were written in my notebook and for my journey, so I thanked them. Half a month had passed since the beginning of my pilgrimage. The end of autumn had come and I felt the cold.

I had breakfast with the priest's family. I tried to give the priest an offering, but he gave it back to me and said, "Money is very important for your journey, so it is better that you keep it." He did not speak much but he was filled with love. I was deeply impressed by him. He worried about where I would go next, so he called and arranged for me to call on a family he knew and gave me a map with directions to their house. The priest told the Suzuki family I would visit them at noon and asked them to please prepare lunch.

I took a little bit of a roundabout way because I wanted to see Fuji-san from Enshunada, a beautiful viewpoint. I walked toward Iwata, hoping to reach the Suziki house by noon. At 9:45 I crossed the Tendu-gawa. The river was so wide I could not see the end of the bridge. It took me fifteen minutes to walk across the bridge on the pedestrian walkway. In the middle I stopped and looked down. The water was dark blue and clear. The river was very low with many rapids because there was a dam upstream.

A little before noon I was still walking. I searched for the fire lookout tower in the town but I could not find it. Finally I found the Suzuki house. It was already 1 o'clock. They had prepared a big lunch and waited one hour for me even though they did not know me. I thought it was too much for me alone, but I was walking for Buddha so I thanked them and ate. Usually I only had a quick lunch of pastry but today's lunch was very delicious and I thought my stomach must be very surprised. After I rested for half an hour the kind family saw me off and I continued walking.

There was not much traffic in the city so I could walk easily. On both sides of the river there was a windbreak of pine trees but I could still feel the wind blowing through the trees. Maybe in places like this the heroic Jirocho family, who had helped the poor people, would walk with their shoulders thrust forward, breaking the wind. The road continued, with golden stalks of rice bending their heads on either side. I could see people working in the fields far away, cutting the rice.

A small stone Jizō, the deity who helps children, stood on the side of the road wearing a red baby bib. The name of an eight-year-old girl was carved on this Jizō and there were fresh flowers in front of the statue. Perhaps she had died in an accident. I prayed for her in front of the Jizō.

I did not have a reservation for a ryokan that night and the houses were becoming fewer and farther apart. The sun was already setting and the lights were coming on. I stopped at one house and asked if there was an inn nearby. They said there was one in the next town, Yaojin. I had to walk another half hour. I was already tired so I tried to cheer myself up. At last I arrived at the inn. I was exhausted. This ryokan looked so old I thought perhaps a servant would come with a bucket of water to wash my feet, the way they did in ancient times when people traveled by foot wearing *waraji*, straw sandals.

I was an unexpected customer but they were very polite and took me to a room. I spoke with the owner of the ryokan, a lady who was nearly seventy years old, telling her about my journey.

She said, "Please forgive me. It's very noisy in the next room, but I want to talk to you about my son and my life." A party was going on but the woman talked until midnight. I wanted to listen to her story all night long.

Before the Great Pacific War, when her son was eighteen, he volunteered to go to Manchuria to cultivate the land, which was controlled by the Japanese government at that time. While he was there the war started and he was drafted into the army. He was sent to Siberia and died there. She was crying because she had not been able to take care of her son. Her old face full of sorrow, she said, "His friend told me the reason he might have died in the war. Every night the soldiers drew straws to see who would go out to steal food. One night my son was chosen to go out and did not return, so perhaps he was killed by a farmer in the area. The government sent me a white box but there were no bones inside, so no one knew how or where he died. He was an unfortunate boy."

I said to her, "Your son died for the lives of his fellow soldiers. His sacrifice made him *bosatsu*, a servant of life. I am sure he is with Buddha now." I made up a poem for mothers who lost their son in the war and recited it for her.

*sen'yu no*
*kate o motomete*
*senjyo ni*
*chirishi sonomi wa*
*bosatsu narubeshi*

In the war
you tried to find food
for your friends
and died on the battleground.
You are a servant of life

隊

戦友の糧をもとめて

戦場に斃れ

その身は

菩薩なりせし

有

The old woman was very happy. Before, she thought her son's death had no meaning but now she could think of his death in a new light. Because he died for someone else he was godly. "Thank you very much," she said.

I too felt happy. I had a wonderful experience in this ryokan.

# DAY 16 (21 OCTOBER)
## OSUGACHU TO SAGARA

Early in the morning the hotel owner came with *hanshi* paper and calligraphy materials and asked me to write the poem I had recited last night. She said, "This poem will be my treasure. If I don't meet you again my thinking will never change. Now I feel I've woken up."

In my notebook I wrote her son's name and told her I would pray for him at the temple at Shimizu. She had tears in her eyes.

In the morning it was raining hard. But when it was time to go the weather cleared up. It was strange the way it would rain at night but be fine in the morning. Perhaps Buddha was protecting me. There were many shade trees on either side of the road so it was nice for walking.

I came to a place where steep stone steps led up to a shrine. In front of the steps there was a big stone with the name of the shrine and on the back the name of the stone mason, Hayashi Senjūrō. I had met him. He was a relative of my mother. It was a surprise to see his name there. Hayashi had been the head of the army during the war so perhaps many soldiers came to pray at this shrine. I rested beside the stone for about twenty minutes. There was nobody there and no cars passed. I wanted to climb the steps but I did not have much time, so I looked up at the shrine and clapped my hands three times in the traditional Shinto custom.

I began walking again. It was Saturday and the students were going home. Kindergarten children were walking in a line along the busy road. Many older students rode bicycles. In front of me, two students wearing long-sleeved uniforms walked with short steps. They looked like seventh-grade students. As I walked behind them, one of them turned toward me and I smiled. They must have thought I was very strange because they walked faster. I also walked faster. They walked even faster. Finally they both ran away, swinging their heavy school bags. I stopped teasing them but they had already disappeared.

I arrived at Jitougata, which had been my destination on my original schedule. I tried to find a ryokan but this town was too small, so I walked on for more than an hour, coming to Sagara at sunset. It was a sad village with few people. I opened the front door of a ryokan and a woman asked, "Are you alone?" She was wearing heavy makeup. I thought this inn might be special. I had no partner so I could not stay there.

I left and tried to find another inn. I decided that I would take what I could find whether it was good or not. The next ryokan had seen better days. At one time it had been a nice inn but now it was falling apart. Not many people would stay there but it was getting dark. *Shikata ga nai*, I thought, it could not be helped. It was better than sleeping outside. The innkeeper was a bit scruffy. He said, "Just stay anywhere you like." It was a big inn but there were no other customers around.

I decided to stay on the second floor because it was a bit cleaner, in the room closest to the front door. The room was damp and there was only one dirty *zabuton* for sitting on the floor. The fusuma were broken and did not close properly. I had to slam them to get them closed. A woman came, carrying a tray of tea for me. Her hair was messy and covered with a towel. Without saying anything she set down the tray.

The bath was decrepit, with one weak light. I could see through the window, which meant people could see inside, so I hurried back to the room without taking off my clothes or washing. The futon were dirty so I slept in my clothes and I only put the comforter up to my chest and used my towel near my face. I could not relax.

In the middle of the night there was a big crash. I heard the sound of the front door opening. It sounded like two or three men were coming in. I thought they might be traveling salesmen. I was nervous because the fusuma had no lock. What should I do? There was nothing protecting me. So I took the fusuma off the closet and put it against the fusuma to the hall so no one could open it. Then I sat there quietly listening. I heard heavy footsteps coming up the stairs, clunk, clunk. But they went into a different room. I knew I was probably safe, but still I could not sleep and I stayed awake all night long.

I had stayed in the ryokan of my choice until now but this broken-down inn was not the kind of lodging I would choose. But there were *tatami* mats and futon, and I had food. It was enough for me. If I did not have a place to sleep and food to eat, what would I do? Maybe Buddha was giving me the opportunity to change my desire for luxury. I wrote a haiku about this experience.

*yuki kurete*
*koson no aki no*
*nami makura*


Autumn dusk, difficult to arrive –
a sad village with few people.
Pillowed on the sound of waves.

行き行きて
たふれ伏すとも
萩の原
〳〵

After putting so much effort into walking all that way, finally darkness came and I could rest. Listening to the sound of the waves was like resting on a *zafu*, a soft meditation pillow. I felt pillowed on the sound of the waves.

# DAY 17 (22 OCTOBER)
## SAGARA TO SHIZUOKA

Last night I slept on a cold futon and did not sleep much. I got up at 4:30. It was still dark outside. I waited until dawn and started to walk at 6:30. I had already paid for my room so I went out without saying anything. I walked, stretching my arms above my head and breathing deeply. Today was Sunday so there were many fishermen on the shore. With so many fishing lines the fish must have been confused. I crossed over Ōi-gawa. This bridge was also long but there was no fee. The bridge shook from the passing of many cars, bouncing me up and down. In ancient times people said, "You could cross Hakone-yama by horse but you could not cross Ōi-gawa because there was too much water." Nowadays there was not much water and I felt sad.

I stopped for a rest in the town of Katahama, where I saw a demolished car. It was so damaged I thought maybe people had died in a *jidōsha jiko*. I prayed in front of the car. Human life is transient, I thought. I am fine right now but any moment I could die. The more people use cars for convenience, the more dangerous life will become. We must live each moment with great care.

An old man, about eighty years old, came toward me. I asked him whether someone had died in this car accident. He said, "There have been four or five accidents in this place, so we put up a Jizō for the people who died but still another accident happened." He sat down on an empty wooden box on the shore and offered me a seat. He asked about my trip.

I told him, "I am walking for the people who died in the war. Today is the seventeenth day."

The old man listened with his head bowed. When he looked up at me, his sunburned and deeply creased face was covered with tears. Suddenly I realized he had lost someone in the war. A moment later he said, "I can see Izu peninsula on the sea, Fuji-san to the east. I have enjoyed my long life in tranquility." Then he told me, "My name is Morita Taido. I am a twenty-eighth-generation descendent of an assistant to the daimyō of Shizuoka-ken. I was a Tōkyō palace guard. My ancestors were great but I did not have good fortune. In the war my brother died in Taiwan and my son died in Singapore. Now I am in my eighties but I still feel sad for them." The old man looked at me with tears in his eyes. "Many people bow to me. I do not bow to anyone. But now I bow to you with all my heart. I pray for your safe journey and hope you will complete your trip for the people who died in the war." He bowed deeply to me.

I also bowed to him because I felt he had given me too much respect. I left him sitting on the box. When I looked back he kept waving at me for a long time. There was no chance to meet him again but I would never forget what happened that day. He would remain in my heart forever.

*komiageru*
*namida koraete*
*gouchoku no*
*yasoji no okina*
*yukisi ko kataru*

Remembering his son,
he tried to stop the tears.
The old man was in his eighties,
seemingly strong but soft inside.
He talked about his son
who died in the war.

一
み
め
希
の
涙
こ
ら
を
し
剛
直
の
心
路
の
治
行
き
て
子
語
り

# DAY 18 (23 OCTOBER)
# SHIZUOKA TO SHIMIZU

I hurried to Nihondaida, without any breakfast as usual. Looking at the hill from far away, I thought it was not so high but the road up was very long. There was another toll gate. The toll road I walked on a few days ago had many trees and bushes with a valley on one side but this was only a wide grassy hill. I reached a viewpoint at the top but it was a pity that I could not see Fuji-san because of the fog. The road going down was smooth and there were mikan orchards and tea fields on both sides of the road. Soon the fog lifted and I could see the Bay of Suruga.

After three and a half hours I reached the foot of the hill and was already in Shimizu City, the birthplace of Shimizu no Jirocho, the legendary folk hero and undefeated swordsman. His bones were interred in Beiin-ji, a Zen temple. There was a statue of him in the temple garden and in the little exhibition hall I saw the clothes, swords and cups that had belonged to him and his wife. At his grave site I found something very interesting. Many people had chipped his gravestone to take a memory of this great, kind man, hoping to be like him. But now we could not get close because there was a fence around the grave.

Next door was Ryuge-ji, the grave site of the famous author Takayama Chogyū, who influenced Japanese literature during the late Meiji period. In the garden there was a big, old cycad tree, a natural monument. The bent tree trunk looked like an elephant's trunk. Higher up was a stone garden with a statue of Takayama. He was a follower of the Buddhist sect, Nichiren, and he loved Fuji-san.

Since I was so close to Mihonomatsubara, a famous row of pine trees protecting the road from the sea wind, I decided to go that way even though it was a longer distance. On the way many trucks passed me carrying big logs to make paper pulp so I walked on the beach. It was hard to walk in the sand. At last I arrived at Mihonomatsubara and I could see Fuji-san over the sea. I recalled the story of the angel's shawl. It is said that an angel came from heaven to the seaside. She was wearing a flowing shawl, which got caught on a pine tree. A passing fisherman untangled it but he did not want to give it back to her. She danced beautifully for him and he finally returned the shawl. Then she was able to go back to heaven.

I stood looking at this scene for a little while, my heart filled with deep silence. After I finish this journey, I thought, my life will be changed from silence to busy activity. A sight-seeing bus arrived and many people took pictures in front of this famous pine tree. A little wave washed over my feet. I picked up a small stone as a souvenir and left. I went back the same way I had come and hurried to Monyou-ji.

In the evening I arrived at the temple at last. The last time I sat down in front of an image of Buddha was three days ago. As I prayed before the statue of Buddha once more, I remembered the proud old man's face in Sagara, covered with tears.

# DAY 19 (24 OCTOBER)
# SHIMIZU TO FUJISHI

Dawn was late because it was late autumn. In the main room
the praying had already started. I sat behind the priest for
two hours and prayed with him. My notebook was in front
of the Buddha so I felt sure that the many people who died in
the war would be happy. I had breakfast and the priest's wife
made a box lunch for me.

I set out along Route 1 to the east. The road became narrow
and there was a lot of traffic. The cars drove slowly, filling the
air with fumes, and I put a handkerchief over my nose. This
road was not good for pedestrians and I felt a little unhappy. I
found a small road and turned that way. The air was clear. I
looked at the handkerchief. The white cotton had two black
holes where my nostrils had been. But then the little road
came back to Route 1 and the cars went by slowly like cows.

I arrived at the Oda family house. Looking out the window
I could see Fuji-san. The mountain looked like it was right in
front of me. I thought they must be happy to live in a place
like this. The wife was very kind. I thought of the sutra that
says the Buddha changes his body to human form to help
people, so that family was the Buddha. I thanked them very
much for taking care of me. At night we talked and I had a
very nice time with them.

# DAY 20 (25 OCTOBER)
# FUJISHI TO NUMAZU

Last night we talked about our religion and I heard about their experiences. Oda-san said, "Humans don't always have good circumstances so we must live the right way. Only then will we succeed." He was the president of a big company. Every morning and evening he prayed to a statue of the Buddha in his room. I thought his employees must be happy that they had such a good employer.

I looked outside. This place was at the foot of Fuji-san. Even though the weather was cloudy I could see the sacred mountain, covered with snow on top.

Starting out I looked at the map and walked along Route 1 once more. Too much traffic, I hated it. It might be further but I chose a smaller road. A typhoon was coming and the weather was getting worse but it was still good for walking. Later I encountered construction for the new Tomei Expressway, with many dump trucks passing by.

At noon I bought bread and milk in a shop. The owner asked, "Where are you going?"

"I am walking from Kyōto to Tōkyō," I replied, "praying for the people who died in the war."

She was surprised to hear I had walked all the way from Kyōto and asked me to sit on a zabuton and talk. She told me, "My brother also died in the war. I don't always remember him because I'm so busy. You are walking and praying for many people who died in the war, including my brother. I feel sorry that I don't remember him often so thank you for what you're doing."

We told stories about the war and life after the war. She gave me apples and sweets, saying, "Please eat them when you feel hungry. I will pray for my brother and others who died from now on."

I decided to pray for the woman's brother at the temple where I would be staying that night. Again I thought of the saying, ichi go ichi e. I have all these memories of meeting with people yet I have only met them one time in my life. I felt I was saying sayōnara to someone I knew very well.

I walked on the beach. I could still see the row of pine trees far in the distance. After awhile I arrived at Hara. This place was on the old Tōkaidō. Pine trees lined the road so people called this Senbonmatsubara, Thousand Pine Trees Row. I walked along this road, looking at the sea blowing in the wind, until I reached Numazu.

I found Monpō-ji easily so I arrived earlier than I had expected. Two priests with many believers welcomed me warmly. Hayashi-san looked after me from my arrival until my departure. I was very happy.

# DAY 21 (26 OCTOBER)
# NUMAZU TO ASHINO-KO

We talked together until late at night. Early in the morning Hayashi-san prepared breakfast for me. I was so happy. The Hayashis took a picture of me with their family, which they would send to me later. I did not want to say goodbye but I left the temple.

Today I would cross Hakone-yama. This would be a test of endurance. Until now the weather had been fine, raining at night but clearing by morning. But now that I was going to cross the Hakone range a typhoon was coming and the weather had turned strange. Even though the weather was getting worse I decided to keep to my original plan to reach Ashino-ko, the crater lake, that day. I was a little worried but then I thought, I am traveling with Buddha so I do not need to worry.

I took courage and walked to Mishima, at the foot of Hakone-yama. The road started gradually going up. Route 1 had too much traffic. I took a side road but after awhile it rejoined Route 1. Looking back I could see the town of Mishima below. In front of me were many mountains forming a ring around the ancient Hakone caldera, with dark clouds descending on the peaks.

The road went into a forest and the air became cool. Under a big tree there was a statue of Batō Kannon, a special Kannon for animals. It was very rare because instead of just a rock with the inscription, Batō Kannon, it was a statue of a human body with a fierce face and the head of a horse in the crown. I prayed in front of the statue and thought of the horses, dogs and messenger pigeons that died in the war. Yes, humans died in this war but also animals. I had not thought of that until now. I felt very sorry for them. Who prayed for those animals, which worked very hard in battle without complaining and died for the people? I prayed many times for them with great care. After that I left.

No one was walking on this road so the drivers looked at me with surprise. The truck drivers were used to being kind to hitchhikers and one of them offered me a ride. But my journey was a pilgrimage so I had to walk. Cars often passed me and I wondered if the exhaust fumes would kill the cherry trees. The buds were covered with black soot and had not bloomed even though it was already autumn. The thistle flowers were also blackened. But the mountains far away were beautiful, covered with golden leaves.

I walked up around many curves but I did not arrive at the top. I could see a bus driving far above on the mountain road. It looked like a toy. I had to go up there but my feet felt heavy. The road had been climbing since morning. I walked very hard until noon. Then I sat on the grass and ate onigiri, which the priest's wife had given me that morning. There were no hikers around here. I walked again, singing the Hakone-yama song, heading for the next mountain, but when I arrived there was another mountain. I wondered how I would ever reach the top. Usually I could walk four kilometers an hour but now I could not even walk three.

Suddenly a truck stopped beside me. A middle-aged man asked me, "Where are you going? I saw you before."

I answered, "To Ashino-ko."

"It's a ways yet to Ashino-ko, so please get in."

"My journey is for pilgrimage so I cannot get in but thank you for your offer."

"Take care," he said and drove away.

The sun was setting but I still had not reached the top. The same truck driver came and stopped his truck beside me. He said, "You won't reach the top until after the sun sets so I will take you."

What should I do? But this was also Buddha's help, so I said, "All right, please take me a little while but when I see the top I will walk again." I did not feel comfortable accepting a ride in the truck because I felt obliged to walk to the lake at the top.

After I got out of the truck I walked another hour to the top. This kind driver always drove this way from Chiba prefecture and I thanked him. I arrived at Ashino-ko before sunset. It was getting dark and I could hear the sound of the typhoon. I felt ill at ease. Walking along the *sugi namiki*, a row of Japanese cedars, I arrived at Ashino-ko at 6 o'clock in the evening, two hours later than my schedule. I chose a ryokan nearest to the road. I had finished this day's long trip, climbing up the whole day. My legs were tired, as usual. I massaged them as I soaked in the o-furo but they did not recover.

# DAY 22 (27 OCTOBER) ASHINO-KO TO ODAWARA

Early in the morning I woke up to the sound of the storm beating against the glass window. In the news they said the *taifū* would pass the Izu peninsula today. Looking out at Ashino-ko, sightseeing boats were rolling up and down and pitching back and forth in the gale. I wondered whether I should go into the fierce *arashi* or not, but I felt Buddha was testing me so I decided to go. After breakfast I put on a raincoat. The people in the ryokan said not to go, but if I took a rest for a day my pilgrimage would be useless so I left the inn.

The rain pushed me from the side so hard I could hardly walk. I used my umbrella like a shield. When the road changed directions the wind came from behind, pushing me hard. The kasa went inside out so I could not use it anymore. The heavy rain made the sound, *zā-zā*, and my shoes in the water made the sound, *jabo-jabo*. The rain was like a waterfall on my raincoat. My body was wet to the skin and my stomach hurt. I walked fast, thinking of warm food on my arrival in the town. The road became like a river. The flow of water was so strong it had washed away all the sand that filled the little holes in the road so the going was rough. The soles of my shoes were getting thin and would soon be full of holes but I had vowed to use the same shoes until I reached Tōkyō.

I saw a bus stop and thought about taking a bus because I was so tired and wet. But I knew I must keep walking and anyway I realized the bus would not come because of the typhoon. Instead of waiting I walked down further. The rain grew a little weaker. The golden leaves made beautiful patterns on the road. When the weather cleared the cars would come again and the beautiful patterns would disappear at once. I enjoyed the scenery for a while, all alone.

The storm was ending and the road became flat. Now Hakone Yumoto was near. The sun was shining through the clouds with soft beams. It was so strange. I could not believe the typhoon had vanished so suddenly. I was being strengthened through the trials of this pilgrimage. Moved, I wiped away tears of gratitude.

I found an *udon* shop so I dashed inside. No other customers were there.

The owner of the noodle shop was surprised and said, "What happened to you?"

I told him about my journey since that morning.

He was astonished and said, "Change your clothes quickly. Otherwise you'll get a cold."

Then he took me to another room where I could change into my dry clothes. Once more I had the good fortune to meet kind people. The noodles were warm. I recovered my energy, thanked him and walked from Yumoto toward Odawara.

This road was the same one I passed a month ago by car on another trip and I compared the power of the human with the power of the machine. At 3 o'clock I arrived at the Kojima house in Odawara, which was also a hair salon. The sun was still high in the sky. The daughter washed and set my hair. In the evening I had a wonderful dinner with the family and went to bed early. I recalled the day's suffering and the joy of passing through it. I also learned a lot about human kindness. It became a good memory.

# DAY 23 (28 OCTOBER)
# ODAWARA TO HIRATSUKA

In the morning the youngest daughter came back from a school trip and we all heard her story. Her manner was polite and she was also pretty. After breakfast I left the house. Today I planned to go to Hiratsuka. The distance was not far. I walked along Route 1 a little while and then I remembered that I had forgotten my umbrella. I phoned them. The daughter brought it to me by bicycle. I thought I might still need an umbrella sometime.

Suddenly an ambulance went past me and stopped just ahead. I hurried there and looked. An old woman about eighty years old had fallen down unconscious. She might have been walking alone through the town and had no relations nearby. Soon people gathered but no one knew her. She was carried by stretcher into the ambulance. We never know what will happen to us. It reminded me of the expression, *shogyo mujo*, all is vanity. I prayed for her to recover.

Around Kōzu the sea is nearby. I could see big white waves on my right, which called me to the seashore, so I took the road to the coast. The waves were still very high because of the typhoon yesterday. They came toward me, surging up and down and crashing into each other. I gazed at the scenery for a while because I love the waves.

When I looked at the horizon I saw a ship. It quickly went below the horizon but it was still floating. I suddenly realized that I could not see the ship because the earth is round. Anyone standing on the shore could see the horizon but could not see beyond the horizon. No one could see that far even if that person was rich or famous. In that way everyone is equal. I suddenly understood the fundamental condition of human life. This insight was satori, a spiritual awakening for me. Up to the horizon is in this world but beyond the horizon is Buddha's realm. Our spiritual practice has a purpose but when we reach that goal we find another one beyond that. We never reach the final destination.

From Ninomiya I walked to Ōiso. Long ago, Yoshida, the prime minister of Japan, lived in this town and built the road to Tōkyō. I arrived at Jyogyo-ji in Hiratsuka at 4 o'clock. It was already getting dark. This was the last temple I would stay in on this journey. I greeted the priest and left the notebook in front of the temple's statue of Buddha. I stayed in the Yoshida family's house that night. They had been in Nara before so I thought of them with affection. The priest's wife made dinner for me and I gratefully ate the meal.

# DAY 24 (29 OCTOBER)
# HIRATSUKA TO HARAMACHIDA

At the Yoshida family house they served breakfast at 6 o'clock. I thanked them for their warm hospitality and went back to Jogyo-ji. At the main temple the head priest, Kawade Nisho, in a scarlet *reifuku* indicating high rank, was chanting a sutra. In front of him was my notebook, which he prayed over. I sat behind him and prayed quietly for the victims of war. Tomorrow I would be in Tōkyō. This would be the last prayer session at a temple on my pilgrimage. Through my prayers I hoped the war dead would rest in peace. After the prayers the priest returned the notebook to me. I told him the story about the events yesterday at the Kōzu coast. The priest said, "That is your Buddha wisdom. It is the result of your pilgrimage." And he wrote a message in my notebook: "Your hope has been achieved."

The Yoshida couple also came to the temple and said sayōnara to me. With many thanks to them, I started toward the east. Later I crossed the bridge over the Banyu-gawa. When I looked back I could see beautiful Fuji-san under the autumn sky and I could also see Hakone-yama. This experience of crossing the Hakone Mountains during a typhoon was the greatest treasure of my life. It had been very difficult but now it was a good memory. I realized how all my experiences become just a memory. Only two days had passed but it already seemed like a long time ago.

The Fuji-san I could see now was on the opposite side of where I had stayed at the Oda family's house in Fujishi. I had walked all the way around to the far side of the sacred mountain. Once more I started walking. I walked and walked but I could not find any shops. While I was taking a short rest, the long white body of the shinkansen streaked by in a flash. Again I calculated the time and distance I usually walked in a day compared with the shinkansen, which could cover the same distance in just ten minutes. People must think my walk is very silly or pointless, I thought. I am a rare person to make such a journey on foot. But for me this was the first and last chance in my life. Only Buddha could understand my pilgrimage.

After a while I found a shop at Ayase where I could buy bread and milk. The woman who owned the shop looked at me with curiosity. I said I would be in Tōkyō tomorrow and told her the story of my travels. She was another war widow. She was so impressed with my story she refused payment for the food. She also gave me a few tangerines and persimmons. I was very happy that she understood my pilgrimage.

I looked for a ryokan. In the first one, I found a few noisy American soldiers with Japanese girls so I left quickly. This place was really close to Atsugi Army Base, with many soldiers wandering around. I heard that every inn was like this so I decided to go to Enoshima. It might be far from here but I had to go there.

Today was Sunday and most ryokan were closed but I went to a big inn and found a room. Even though the town was very crowded with travelers I had a big room all to myself and I could relax.

# DAY 25 (30 OCTOBER)
# HARAMACHIDA TO TŌKYŌ

Today was finally the last day. I woke up earlier in the morning because I had to return to the road at Haramachida, far from where I had stayed last night. I left at 7 o'clock and went back to my starting point, which took one hour.

There were rice fields on either side of the river. It was the harvest season but after the typhoon the stalks of ripe grain had fallen down into the waterlogged fields and turned black. I remembered the beautiful flat rice fields at Omiheia, twenty days ago. In that area the people worked only as farmers so the power of agriculture was strong there. But in this place the farmers sometimes worked at another job and I did not feel the same power of agriculture. I felt sorry for these rice fields. There was a lack of agricultural manpower here because they could only cut the rice on Sunday. We can get good results only when we focus on one thing.

At the border of the prefecture I found a sign board, City of Tōkyō. At last I had entered Tōkyō. I was within two hours of my final destination. I stood and stared at the sign board. My twenty-five days of walking from Kyōto through Shiga, Gifu, Aichi, Shizuoka and Kanagawa prefectures would soon be finished and all my troubles had changed to good memories.

I walked through the landscape of rice fields. After that the number of houses increased and I could see familiar names, a sign that I was getting closer to Tōkyō. I knew the places around here and I felt I had almost reached my goal. I sat down on the bank of the Tama-gawa and took the persimmons and tangerines from my rucksack, preparing to eat them. Some construction workers sat down to eat lunch close near me and I gave them the fruit instead of eating it myself. They were very happy.

I crossed the bridge over the river and walked beside the railway line toward to Shibuya. When I was an elementary school student I used to walk to the Tama-gawa to play. It made me feel very nostalgic. Who would ever guess that I would walk the same road on a pilgrimage? No one knows the future. Compared to the old days the town looked very busy, full of many people and shops. I began walking faster and forgot my travel fatigue.

At Josen-ji, the last temple on my pilgrimage, I greeted the priest, asked him to write in my notebook and gave thanks for safely completing my journey. My travels were over at last but I did not feel any deep emotion at all. I do not know why. Every day my purpose had been to walk to Tōkyō. Finally when I arrived in Tōkyō my purpose was gone. At the start no one had been there to see me off and in Tōkyō no one was there when I arrived. I did not speak to any of my family or friends the day I returned. Instead I sat in the main temple with a feeling of deep serenity. My journey seemed long but at the same time short and now it was over. My heart was calm and quiet. I sat there remembering my journey, which was both a distant memory and fresh in my awareness.

I had walked from west to east for twenty-five days. The right side of my face was tanned and the color of my left and right hands was different. This contrast was a good memory for me. I went to the post office and sent over thirty telegrams to let my family and friends know of my safe arrival. A newspaper reporter from the *Asahi Shimbun* showed up but I said, "No, no, no, no, I do not want to be in the newspaper."

Then I returned to my home in Nara, a three-hour trip by shinkansen. At dinner that night they served a big sea bream fish in celebration of my safe return. I was filled with great satisfaction. I would never be able to do this kind of pilgrimage again and I felt deep appreciation for the many people who supported me and the many people I met during my journey.

One week after I got back to Nara, I went to Jakko-in, the number one sub-temple of Hie-zan, which is the main temple where all the Tendaishu monks do their training. My teacher, Komatsu-chiko, the head nun, made *sekihan*, sweet sticky rice with red beans used for special celebrations, and many other special dishes in honor of my return. She gave me a *kesa*, a special red and gold silk stole. The color is very special. Believers usually wear other colored kesa but I received one signifying the highest rank.

# ABOUT THE AUTHORS

**Goto Hiroko**

Goto Hiroko is a tea ceremony and traditional calligraphy master. She lives in Oshino-mura, Yamanashi-ken, Japan, where she teaches and promotes humanitarian causes.

**Care Connet**

Care Connet holds master's degrees in history and professional writing. She lives in Fairfield, Iowa, U.S.A., where she writes, paints, photographs and participates in world peace programs.

www.ingramcontent.com/pod-product-compliance
Lightning Source LLC
LaVergne TN
LVHW091227080426
835509LV00009B/1200